Lessons from

JOSEPH

Andrew Wommack

Published in partnership between Andrew Wommack Ministries and Harrison House Publishers.

Woodland Park, CO 80863 – Shippensburg, PA 17257

ISBN 13 TP: 978-1-5954-8561-8

For Worldwide Distribution, Printed in the USA

1 / 26 25 24 23

Introduction

Without a doubt, one of the greatest examples of character in Scripture is the Old Testament saint Joseph. He faced challenges and adversity that most people have never experienced. And yet, very few people in the history of the world have made as much of an impact, not only on one nation but multiple nations. You may be at a place where you're wondering, *God, how do I get from where I am to where I'm supposed to be?* Well, Joseph went from the pit to the palace in less than twenty-four hours! Now, there was a thirteen-year incubation period before all of this happened. But there are things you can learn through him that would save you from making the mistakes so many Christians make.

Some people say, "You can't really know what a person is going through until you've gone through it yourself." In other words, you have to experience the same hurts and the same troubles as somebody else in order to learn from them. No, if you go to the school of hard knocks, it makes a great testimony if you survive it. But I don't recommend it. You can learn through your own mistakes, or you can learn through someone else's.

Everything that was recorded in the Old Testament was for our benefit so that we would learn what to do and what not to do. (1 Cor. 10:6–11) You can live vicariously through Joseph and apply his example to your life.

If you've been given promises from God and yet your circumstances don't seem to line up, I want to encourage you to learn from Joseph. If you will receive these things that I'll be sharing, this has the potential to change your life!

Who is Joseph?

Joseph is a young man in the Bible who was given dreams of greatness from God. The Bible reveals how he carried himself and how he held on to what God gave even though he faced many challenges. He was the eleventh of twelve sons of Jacob and is one of two sons born to Rachel, the wife whom Jacob loved the most. That's pretty much all the background you get about Joseph before his story really takes off in Genesis 37, where we'll begin reading.

> "These are the generations of Jacob. Joseph, being seventeen years old, was feeding the flock with his brethren . . .. Now Israel loved Joseph more than all his children, because he was the son of his old age: and he made him a coat of many colours. And when his brethren saw that their father loved him more than all his brethren, they hated him, and could not speak peaceably unto him."
>
> Genesis 37:2–4

This hatred that Joseph's brothers had for him was not caused by him. It was his father who occasioned this animosity because of his preferential treatment of Joseph.

However, the backstory of Joseph's brothers reveals that these were evil men (Gen. 34–35 and 38).

Genesis 37:5 says,

"And Joseph dreamed a dream, and he told it his brethren: and they hated him yet the more."

Notice that Joseph's brothers hated him even more. Speaking forth his dreams exacerbated the situation. The only flaw that you might be able to attribute to Joseph is a lack of wisdom and maturity in telling people who hated him what God had put in his heart. But, as the story will bear out, it's actually more plausible that he just believed in his dream enough to share it. Faith talks (2 Cor. 4:13). So, first off, when you have a dream and you know it's from the Lord, the correct response is to choose to believe it.

> Lesson 1:
>
> **When you have a dream and you know it's from the Lord, the correct response is to choose to believe it.**

Now, you need to be careful about sharing what God has shown you. Jesus said not to cast your pearls before swine (Matt. 7:6). You could inadvertently draw criticism and unbelief from those who don't understand. But Joseph was probably so excited about what God had shown him that he just blurted it out. To just label him as spoiled and arrogant is inconsistent with the character he shows not long after this and throughout his life.

Lesson 2:
You need to be careful about sharing what God has shown you.

Now let's read the details of this dream he had:

"And he said unto them, Hear, I pray you, this dream which I have dreamed: For, behold, we were binding sheaves in the field, and, lo, my sheaf arose, and also stood upright; and, behold, your sheaves stood round about, and made obeisance to my sheaf."

Genesis 37:6–7

This was symbolic of the way that all of Joseph's brothers would someday come and bow down to him. Look what happened next in verse 8:

"And his brethren said to him, Shalt thou indeed reign over us? or shalt thou indeed have dominion

5

over us? And they hated him yet the more for his dreams, and for his words."

Joseph's brothers understood this dream, and man, was it offensive to them! They probably looked at him and remembered him as a little kid with a runny nose. They didn't see anything special. They knew all of the wrong things he'd done. Now he's claiming that God is going to use him.

Most people just want everybody to be like them. In a sense, it justifies their mediocre life. But when someone comes along and says, "No, I'm going to be different. The power of God will flow through me," then most people fight against that individual. Rather than humbling themselves and changing, it's easier to criticize and try to pull him down to their level rather than them coming up to the level of the person who wants more out of life. That's exactly what Joseph's brothers did.

Waiting for the Vision

You know, before God uses you, He will always drop a dream in your heart of something bigger and

Lesson 3:

Before God uses you, He will always drop a dream in your heart of something bigger and better than what you are experiencing.

better than what you are experiencing. It doesn't necessarily have to be a dream while you're asleep; it's just a vision, a desire, or a prophecy about what He wants to do with your life. The reason He does this is because you're going to need that dream. You're going to need to hold on to it in the day of trouble. It will give you strength and encouragement between the time that you receive the vision and when it is fulfilled. This is very important.

Speaking of Joseph, Psalm 105:19 says, *"Until the time that his word came: the word of the LORD tried him."*

This is talking about the time that Joseph first received the dreams from God until the time that they came to pass. This is a pattern that God uses with everybody. If Joseph didn't embrace these dreams and operate in faith, he would be griping and complaining when he was being tried. Then the things God showed him wouldn't come to pass.

7

Now let's look at Genesis 37:13–14 and 17–20:

"And Israel said unto Joseph, Do not thy brethren feed the flock in Shechem? come, and I will send thee unto them. And he said to him, Here am I. And he said to him, Go, I pray thee, see whether it be well with thy brethren, and well with the flocks; and bring me word again. So he sent him out of the vale of Hebron, and he came to Shechem . . .. And Joseph went after his brethren, and found them in Dothan. And when they saw him afar off, even before he came near unto them, they conspired against him to slay him. And they said one to another, Behold, this dreamer cometh. Come now therefore, and let us slay him, and cast him into some pit, and we will say, Some evil beast hath devoured him: and we shall see what will become of his dreams."

This is premeditated murder Joseph's brothers were talking about. Even though they didn't follow through with this plot, it was still evil. They settled on selling him to the Ishmeelites, which was just about as evil. It's not recorded here, but later, it says that Joseph pled with them for mercy (Gen. 42:21). They just ignored him. When they returned to their father, they brought back his coat of many colors that they had dipped in goat's blood. They showed it to Jacob and told him Joseph had been killed.

Joseph had a dream from God, yet he was sold into slavery. As a Christian, you're going to face problems in life even if you have a vision from God. During that period of time, this vision will keep you going. Proverbs 29:18 says, *"Where there is no vision, the people perish."*

Lesson 4:

As a Christian, you're going to face problems in life even if you have a vision from God.

True Prosperity

Now let's jump ahead to when Joseph had been sold into slavery. In Genesis 39:1–2, it says,

"And Joseph was brought down to Egypt; and Potiphar, an officer of Pharaoh, captain of the guard, an Egyptian, bought him of the hands of the Ishmeelites, which had brought him down

thither. And the LORD was with Joseph, and he was a prosperous man; and he was in the house of his master the Egyptian."

I think some people just pass over what's being said here, but this is super important. After being stripped of all that was familiar to him—even his clothes—Joseph was standing on an auction block. God looks at him and says he's a prosperous man. That is powerful! The Lord doesn't see things the way that we see them. One of the reasons we get into discouragement, despair, and unbelief is because we don't think the way He thinks. Many of us think we're prosperous based on the value of our houses, cars, clothes, and all of these things. We need to recognize that our prosperity is not tied to our circumstances.

Ephesians 3:20 says, *"Now unto him that is able to do exceeding abundantly above all that we ask or think, according to the power that worketh in us."* God's prosperity is tied to the power that works in you. It's not you doing it without Him; He doesn't move in and through you without your cooperation. Joseph had been given dreams that God was going to exalt him. I believe he held onto that, and it's the reason he was prosperous.

Genesis 39:3–6 says,

"And his master [Potiphar] saw that the LORD was with him, and that the LORD made all that he did to prosper in his hand. And Joseph found grace in his sight, and he served him: and he made him overseer over his house, and all that he had he put into his hand. And it came to pass from the time that he had made him overseer in his house, and over all that he had, that the LORD blessed the Egyptian's house for Joseph's sake; and the blessing of the LORD was upon all that he had in the house, and in the field. And he left all that he had in Joseph's hand."

True prosperity is just the favor of God. But you've got to see it on the inside before you'll see it on the outside. That is a great truth here. You may be in a situation where things don't look good right now, but can you look past that and see the dream that God has put in your heart? Can you walk by faith instead of by sight? Faith is the ability to see things with your heart what

> **Lesson 5:**
> **True prosperity is just the favor of God.**

11

you can't see with your physical eyes. You need to see yourself prosperous. You need to see your marriage working. You need to see your body healed. You need to see these things coming to pass.

Joseph could see that the favor of God was on him, and it was obvious to other people. This does not manifest through a person who's depressed, defeated, and sitting there sucking their thumb and talking about how unfair everything is. For Joseph to prosper like this and be promoted to the head of Potiphar's house, it speaks volumes. It's an indication that he was operating in faith.

If Joseph could believe and he didn't have the baptism of the Holy Spirit, the Bible, and all the things that we have today, then you can believe. He did it with less; certainly we can do it with more.

Excellence

The next part of Genesis 39 says,

"And [Potiphar] knew not ought [Joseph] had, save the bread which he did eat" (v. 6).

So much power was given to Joseph that Potiphar didn't even know what assets he had. Again, this says a lot about the kind of person Joseph was. He had been serving Potiphar so well that he was entrusted with running everything. Even as a slave, he was a faithful steward. I tell you, you are going to have to just start being faithful wherever you are. Jesus said, *"He that is faithful in that which is least is faithful also in much..."* (Luke 16:10) and *"And if ye have not been faithful in that which is another man's, who shall give you that which is your own?"* (v. 12). You have to do things with excellence if you're going to prosper like Joseph did.

> Lesson 7:
> **You have to do things with excellence if you're going to prosper like Joseph did.**

It says in Colossians 3:23,

"And whatsoever ye do, do it heartily, as to the Lord, and not unto men."

Whatever we're doing, we should do it with all of our hearts as if we're serving Christ and not with *"eyeservice, as menpleasers"* (Eph. 6:5). That means we shouldn't work hard only when the boss is looking; we should do it whether man recognizes us or not. God will recognize us.

Let's keep reading.

"...And Joseph was a goodly person, and well favoured" (Gen. 39:6). The NIV translates this as, *"Now Joseph was well-built and handsome."*

"And it came to pass after these things, that his master's wife cast her eyes upon Joseph; and she said, Lie with me."

Genesis 39:7

Before I get into how Joseph replied, let me just say that most people, if they had gone through what he went through, they'd be so bitter and discouraged that they would have given in to this proposition. Joseph could have been tempted to think, *Well, I deserve at least some gratification.* And he probably could have gotten away with it. But Joseph didn't have just situational ethics. The only reason some people have any standard of morality is because of the potential consequences that come if they don't. If that's the only thing that's causing you to do what's right, then I can guarantee you, Satan will present an opportunity where it looks like there won't be any consequences, and you'll just compromise. This happens millions of times. Again, if you're going to prosper, you need to do what's right whether someone is holding you accountable or not.

Lesson 8:
You need to do what's right whether someone is holding you accountable or not.

The next couple of verses say,

"But he refused, and said unto his master's wife, Behold, my master wotteth not what is with me in the house, and he hath committed all that he hath to my hand; There is none greater in this house than I; neither hath he kept back any thing from me but thee, because thou art his wife:

15

how then can I do this great wickedness, and sin against God?"

Genesis 39:8–9

Joseph had a sense of integrity and honor, and he wasn't going to break his master's trust. Joseph had a responsibility to Potiphar, and he had a responsibility to God. Joseph wouldn't dare sin against God because he had such a close relationship with Him. This ought to become a mantra for you: "God, I'm not going to sin against You." If you have a relationship with the Lord, what's important is what He thinks about you, not what others think. The Bible says that *"the integrity of the upright shall guide them"* (Prov. 11:3). What that means is, if you've made a commitment to God, you've put boundaries in your life. That's integrity.

Lesson 9:
Put boundaries in your life.

It's not popular to stand with God and what His Word says. A lot of Christians cave on this because they don't value their relationship with Him like

Lesson 10:
Stand with God and what His Word says.

16

Joseph did. You're missing it if that's you. This is one of the lessons to learn from him, and I just I love this!

It goes on to say,

> *"And it came to pass, as she spake to Joseph day by day, that he hearkened not unto her, to lie by her, or to be with her."*

Genesis 39:10

This is another great thing. Scripture says to flee fornication (1 Cor. 6:18), but then it says to resist the devil and that he will flee from you (James 4:7). You can't just flee from the devil; you have to resist the devil. But you can flee from temptation. Most people are resisting temptation but fleeing from the devil—the exact opposite of what God's Word says. Joseph fled from this master's wife. He refused to even be around her.

Lesson 11:
Resist the devil. Flee temptation.

Genesis 39:11, 16-20 says,

> *"And it came to pass about this time, that Joseph went into the house to do his business; and there*

was none of the men of the house there within. And she [Potiphar's wife] caught him by his garment, saying, Lie with me: and he left his garment in her hand, and fled, and got him out … And she laid up his garment by her, until his lord came home. And she spake unto him according to these words, saying, The Hebrew servant, which thou hast brought unto us, came in unto me to mock me: And it came to pass, as I lifted up my voice and cried, that he left his garment with me, and fled out. And it came to pass, when his master heard the words of his wife, which she spake unto him, saying, After this manner did thy servant to me; that his wrath was kindled. And Joseph's master took him, and put him into the prison, a place where the king's prisoners were bound: and he was there in the prison."

One of the things to notice from this is what didn't happen. Joseph never tried to justify himself against these false accusations. If this had been us, most of us would have gotten the other servants to testify to our integrity. But Joseph didn't say anything. He didn't defend himself. It's possible that as a servant, he didn't have the right—that his master may not have allowed him to speak. Whether that was the case or not, most of us would have been shouting our innocence. Joseph just trusted God to make it right. God said, *"Vengeance is mine; I will repay"* (Rom. 12:19b). You can either let Him defend you, or you can defend yourself. I guarantee you: God can defend you better than you can defend yourself. It may take time, but it will happen.

> Lesson 12:
> # God can defend you better than you can defend yourself.

Prison

So, Potiphar believes the accusations of his wife and has Joseph thrown in prison, which was even worse than being a slave. Our prisons today have flat screen TVs and all of these freedoms. In Joseph's day, conditions were bad in prisons. And yet, the Bible says, *"But the LORD was with Joseph, and shewed him mercy, and gave him favour in the sight of the keeper of the prison"* (Gen. 39:21). Again, one of the lessons to learn from him is that it doesn't matter what things look like on the outside. You have to go by what God has revealed to you in your heart. Everything in the natural is subject to change. That's what it goes on to say:

> "And the keeper of the prison committed to Joseph's hand all the prisoners that were in the prison; and whatsoever they did there, he was the doer of it. The keeper of the prison looked not to any thing that was under his hand; because the LORD was with him, and that which he did, the LORD made it to prosper."
>
> Genesis 39:22–23

Lesson 13:
It doesn't matter what things look like on the outside. Trust what God has revealed to you in your heart.

Lesson 14:
Your promotion will be the result of your faithfulness in the present.

For that jailer to put this kind of responsibility on Joseph, it indicates the kind of attitude Joseph continued to have. He hadn't given up. He was still holding on to what God said. This is one of the greatest lessons to learn from Joseph.

Let's continue into the next chapter.

"And it came to pass after these things, that the butler of the king of Egypt and his baker had offended their lord the king of Egypt. And Pharaoh was wroth against two of his officers, against the chief of the butlers, and against the chief of the bakers. And he put them in ward in the house of the captain of the guard, into the prison, the place where Joseph was bound."

Genesis 40:1–3

We're going to find out that this was divine providence that God had the butler and the baker in the place where Joseph was. The next verse says,

"And the captain of the guard charged Joseph with them, and he served them: and they continued a season in ward" (Gen. 39:4).

Did you know that in Joseph serving these two, it ended up being his ticket out of prison? The lesson here is, if you want to get out of your problems, start ministering to other people. If you feel like you're stuck in a situation but you're not serving anyone, you are cutting off the very people who are your way out. I'm saying this in love, but God is bringing people across your path who could transform your life, and you're missing it because you're just looking at yourself.

Lesson 15:

If you want to get out of your problems, start ministering to other people.

Look at Genesis 40:5–7:

"And they dreamed a dream both of them, each man his dream in one night, each man according to the interpretation of his dream, the butler and the baker of the king of Egypt, which were bound in the prison. And Joseph came in unto them in the morning, and looked upon them, and, behold, they were sad. And he asked Pharaoh's officers that were with him in the ward of his lord's house, saying, Wherefore look ye so sadly to day?"

Again, prisons in those days didn't have the best living conditions. And yet, it was unusual for the butler and the baker to be sad. But notice that this was another opportunity for the power of God to manifest through Joseph:

"And they said unto him, We have dreamed a dream, and there is no interpreter of it. And Joseph said unto them, Do not interpretations belong to God? tell me them, I pray you. And the chief butler told his dream to Joseph, and said to him, In my dream, behold, a vine was before me; And in the vine were three branches: and it was as though it budded, and her blossoms shot forth; and the clusters thereof brought forth ripe grapes: And Pharaoh's cup was in my hand: and I took the grapes, and pressed them into Pharaoh's cup, and I gave the cup into Pharaoh's hand. And Joseph said unto him, This is the interpretation of it: The three branches are three days: Yet within three days shall Pharaoh lift up thine head, and restore thee unto thy place: and thou shalt deliver Pharaoh's cup into his hand, after the former manner when thou wast his butler."

Genesis 40:8–13

Joseph just immediately interpreted the butler's dream. This was supernatural! Then he told the butler, *"But think on me when it shall be well with thee, and shew kindness, I pray thee, unto me, and make mention of me unto Pharaoh, and bring me out of this house"* (Gen. 40:14).

Joseph asked the butler to remember him when he was restored to his position. This is important.

Verses 16–19 say,

"When the chief baker saw that the interpretation was good, he said unto Joseph, I also was in my dream, and, behold, I had three white baskets on my head: And in the uppermost basket there was of all manner of bakemeats for Pharaoh; and the birds did eat them out of the basket upon my head. And Joseph answered and said, This is the interpretation thereof: The three baskets are three days: Yet within three days shall Pharaoh lift up thy head from off thee, and shall hang thee on a tree; and the birds shall eat thy flesh from off thee."

Because the first dream was interpreted in a positive way, the baker thought, *Well, I'll get a positive interpretation too.* But instead, the interpretation predicted disaster. In just three days, he would be beheaded, his body would be hanged on a tree, and the birds would eat his flesh. Again, this speaks to Joseph's integrity. A lot of ministers today would say whatever it takes to tickle people's ears and get a positive response. Joseph didn't do that. He spoke the truth whether he would be received or not. That's powerful.

I also want you to notice that what he interpreted was so specific. Either what he told them was totally from God, or he totally missed it. Joseph knew the Lord was with him, so it gave him boldness to interpret these dreams. It goes on to say,

> *"And it came to pass the third day, which was Pharaoh's birthday, that he made a feast unto all his servants: and he lifted up the head of the chief butler and of the chief baker among his servants. And he restored the chief butler unto his butler-ship again; and he gave the cup into Pharaoh's hand: But he hanged the chief baker: as Joseph had interpreted to them."*
>
> Genesis 40:20–22

Everything came to pass exactly the way Joseph said it would. But then the next verse says,

> *"Yet did not the chief butler remember Joseph, but forgat him"* (v. 23).

The man who was supposed to be Joseph's ticket out forgot about him. The next verse, which is the start of the next chapter (Gen. 41:1), says that two years went by after this. So, Joseph stayed in prison for a couple more years while the butler enjoyed his freedom. This could have been really discouraging for Joseph.

Pharaoh's Dream

Most people—if they had withstood the rejection of their brothers, being sold into slavery, being falsely accused, and put into prison—probably wouldn't be able to survive being forgotten after they had helped somebody. That would've been the end of the story. But at the end of the two years, the Pharaoh had a dream:

"Behold, he stood by the river. And, behold, there came up out of the river seven well favoured kine and fatfleshed; and they fed in a meadow. And, behold, seven other kine came up after them out of the river, ill favoured and leanfleshed; and stood by the other kine upon the brink of the river. And the ill favoured and leanfleshed kine did eat up the seven well favoured and fat kine.

So Pharaoh awoke. And he slept and dreamed the second time: and, behold, seven ears of corn came up upon one stalk, rank and good. And, behold, seven thin ears and blasted with the east wind sprung up after them. And the seven thin ears devoured the seven rank and full ears. And Pharaoh awoke, and, behold, it was a dream."

Genesis 41:1–7

Pharaoh knew that these dreams were significant, and that they were from God. Let's keep reading.

"And it came to pass in the morning that his spirit was troubled; and he sent and called for all the magicians of Egypt, and all the wise men thereof: and Pharaoh told them his dream; but there was none that could interpret them unto Pharaoh. Then spake the chief butler unto Pharaoh, saying, I do remember my faults this day: Pharaoh was wroth with his servants, and put me in ward in the captain of the guard's house, both me and the chief baker: And we dreamed a dream in one night, I and he; we dreamed each man according to the interpretation of his dream. And there was there with us a young man, an Hebrew, servant

to the captain of the guard; and we told him, and he interpreted to us our dreams; to each man according to his dream he did interpret. And it came to pass, as he interpreted to us, so it was; me he restored unto mine office, and him he hanged. Then Pharaoh sent and called Joseph, and they brought him hastily out of the dungeon..."

Genesis 41:8–14

This has to be God's influence upon Pharaoh. You see, even though all of those terrible things had happened to Joseph, the favor of God was still on him. This is a key thing to remember: the gifts and calling of God are without repentance (Rom. 11:29). No one and no thing can cancel it out. You just have to believe it. Through all the hardship Joseph had faced, he still believed.

I also want to draw attention to Genesis 41:14:

"...[Joseph] shaved himself, and changed his raiment, and came in unto Pharaoh."

When Joseph knew he was going before the most important man on the earth, he dressed accordingly. This may seem like a small thing, but I guarantee you, the way you look projects an image. That's not talking about just the way you dress but also your attitude.

Let's read on.

"And Pharaoh said unto Joseph, I have dreamed a dream, and there is none that can interpret it: and I have heard say of thee, that thou canst understand a dream to interpret it. And Joseph answered Pharaoh, saying, It is not in me: God shall give Pharaoh an answer of peace."

Genesis 41:15–16

Joseph didn't say the answer was in him but in God. This is so important. The moment you start trying to take credit and receive glory for what God is doing through you, that will shut off the flow of God's power and anointing.

The next passage says,

"And Pharaoh said unto Joseph, In my dream, behold, I stood upon the bank of the river: And,

29

behold, there came up out of the river seven kine, fatfleshed and well favoured; and they fed in a meadow: And, behold, seven other kine came up after them, poor and very ill favoured and leanfleshed, such as I never saw in all the land of Egypt for badness: And the lean and the ill favoured kine did eat up the first seven fat kine: And when they had eaten them up, it could not be known that they had eaten them; but they were still ill favoured, as at the beginning. So I awoke. And I saw in my dream, and, behold, seven ears came up in one stalk, full and good: And, behold, seven ears, withered, thin, and blasted with the east wind, sprung up after them: And the thin ears devoured the seven good ears: and I told this unto the magicians; but there was none that could declare it to me. And Joseph said unto Pharaoh, The dream of Pharaoh is one: God hath shewed Pharaoh what he is about to do."

Genesis 41:17–25

It doesn't appear that Joseph even hesitated in saying he had the interpretation of Pharaoh's dream. In other words, he didn't have to think about this; he'd been preparing for years. This was the climax of everything he had been believing for. All of us would like to be able to just have the answer in a crisis situation, but the sad fact is, most of us don't seek the Lord until we're *in* a crisis situation.

Lesson 18:

Taking credit for what God is doing through you will shut off the flow of His power and anointing.

"The seven good kine are seven years; and the seven good ears are seven years: the dream is one. And the seven thin and ill favoured kine that came up after them are seven years; and the seven empty ears blasted with the east wind shall be seven years of famine. This is the thing which I have spoken unto Pharaoh: What God is about to do he sheweth unto Pharaoh. Behold, there come seven years of great plenty throughout all the land of Egypt: And there shall arise after them seven years of famine; and all the plenty shall be forgotten in the land of Egypt; and the famine shall consume the land; And the plenty shall not be known in the land by reason of that famine following; for it shall be very grievous . ...

Now therefore let Pharaoh look out a man discreet and wise, and set him over the land of Egypt. Let Pharaoh do this, and let him appoint officers over the land, and take up the fifth part of the land of Egypt in the seven plenteous years. And let them gather all the food of those good years that come, and lay up corn under the hand of Pharaoh, and let them keep food in the cities. And that food shall be for store to the land against the seven years of famine, which shall be in the land of Egypt; that the land perish not through the famine."

Genesis 41:26–31, 33–36

Here, Joseph is telling Pharaoh—the most powerful man on the planet—what he needs to do about this upcoming famine. Only God could promote him like that. If you will serve God and seek Him with your whole heart, He'll make you look good. He'll put you in places and give you authority. The problem with most people is, they tend to think, *God, I can handle it. You just get me introduced, and I can*

> Lesson 19:
>
> **If you will serve God and seek Him with your whole heart, He'll make you look good.**

take it from there. That's the very reason God hasn't used most people.

Joseph was confident in God and sensitive enough to hear His voice to take advantage of this opportunity. Some people are so afraid they'll make a mistake that they would never step out and do what Joseph did. But we can learn from his example here.

The next verses say,

"And the thing was good in the eyes of Pharaoh, and in the eyes of all his servants. And Pharaoh said unto his servants, Can we find such a one as this is, a man in whom the Spirit of God is? And Pharaoh said unto Joseph, Forasmuch as God hath shewed thee all this, there is none so discreet and wise as thou art: Thou shalt be over my house, and according unto thy word shall all my people be ruled: only in the throne will I be greater than thou. And Pharaoh said unto Joseph, See, I have set thee over all the land of Egypt. And Pharaoh took off his ring from his hand, and put it upon Joseph's hand, and arrayed him in vestures of fine linen, and put a gold chain about his neck; And

he made him to ride in the second chariot which he had; and they cried before him, Bow the knee: and he made him ruler over all the land of Egypt. And Pharaoh said unto Joseph, I am Pharaoh, and without thee shall no man lift up his hand or foot in all the land of Egypt."

Genesis 41:37–44

Joseph had literally seized the day! God had put him in a position! No man was going to be able to lift a hand or foot in all of the land of Egypt without his approval. This is just nearly too good to believe!

Trusting God

God has a plan for your life, just as surely as he had a plan for Joseph's life. You might not see it. But if you'll hold on to the dreams God has given you, you could go from the pit to the palace overnight! Everything will work out for you. If you want God to use you, become useable. Start serving other people. He will promote you in due time.

Lesson 20:
God has a plan for your life.

34

If you want God to use you, become useable.

Joseph was now in a position where, if he didn't continue trusting God for favor, Pharaoh could have him killed. There's a lot to be learned here. We not only need to trust God when we're at the bottom, but we need to keep trusting Him after we're on top. A fall from that height would be disastrous.

Now, when Joseph became the most powerful man in Egypt outside of Pharaoh, he had access to the armies. Did you know he could have gone back to his family and made his dreams come to pass? He could have punished them for what they did to him. But he didn't do it. He went through seven years of plenty and two years of the famine and didn't do a thing to make it happen. That has to be the greatest indication of the true heart and character of Joseph.

It's easy to understand how Joseph trusted God when he was a slave and in prison. What other options did he have? Most people, when their backs are against the wall, will turn to God out of desperation. But did you know that success is a greater test of faith than hardship? This is the reason God can't trust some people with promotion. The moment it looks like their crisis is over, they will go back to doing things their own way—to what got them in the crisis in the first place. But once you get promoted, that is a greater temptation for you to quit trusting in God and to think, *I don't have to trust God. Now everything in my life's going good.* More people have been destroyed by prosperity than have ever been destroyed by hardship.

Lesson 22:
Success is a greater test of faith than hardship.

Let's pick up in Genesis 42:1–8:

"Now when Jacob saw that there was corn in Egypt, Jacob said unto his sons, Why do ye look one upon another? And he said, Behold, I have heard that there is corn in Egypt: get you down thither, and buy for us from thence; that we may live, and not die. And Joseph's ten brethren went down to buy corn in Egypt. But Benjamin, Joseph's brother, Jacob sent not with his brethren; for he said, Lest peradventure mischief befall him. And the sons of Israel came to buy corn among those that came: for the famine was in the land of Canaan.

And Joseph was the governor over the land, and he it was that sold to all the people of the land: and Joseph's brethren came, and bowed down themselves before him with their faces to the earth. And Joseph saw his brethren, and he knew them, but made himself strange unto them, and spake roughly unto them; and he said unto them, Whence come ye? And they said, From the land of Canaan to buy food. And Joseph knew his brethren, but they knew not him."

Verse 6 mentions the first of several times Joseph's brothers will bow down to him. After all this time, God's dreams for him are finally starting to come to pass! At this time, all of his brothers, except Benjamin, came down to Egypt to buy food because of the famine. When they got there, Joseph recognized them; but they didn't recognize him.

Spies

I believe that Joseph realized that God was going to use him and his position to bring these evil men to the end of themselves, to see them finally turn to the

Lord. If God hadn't used him to stamp out the evil in his brothers, it would have been reproduced in their children. The nation would have been more wicked than the people in the land of Canaan that God drove out. This was serious. Joseph's actions here weren't punitive at all, but they were corrective.

So, after Joseph asked them about their family, they told him about their father Jacob and their youngest brother Benjamin. Then Joseph basically said, "No, you've come here to spy on us so that you can attack us!" Boy, they were just taken aback by this. Then he, in essence, told them, "This is how I'll know you're not spies. Choose one person to remain here in prison while the rest of you go back to your country. Return with the brother you mentioned. If you can't produce him, then I'll know you were just lying to me." They knew this meant he could have them all killed and started talking amongst themselves:

> "We are verily guilty concerning our brother, in that we saw the anguish of his soul, when he besought us, and we would not hear; therefore is this distress come upon us. And Reuben answered them, saying, Spake I not unto you, saying, Do

not sin against the child; and ye would not hear?
therefore, behold, also his blood is required."

Genesis 42:21–22

Hearing his brothers say this touched Joseph's heart. He probably didn't know that Reuben had planned to come back and save him. It moved Joseph so much that he went into another room and wept. He had to compose himself before coming back. This is not the reaction of a person who's bitter. This is someone who loved his brothers. God was going to use him to break these wicked people and finally have them realize they couldn't prosper living the way they were living. They needed to recognize that there were consequences to their ungodly living.

So, it was decided that Simeon would stay behind while the other nine went home to their father. When Jacob heard what happened, he got mad and basically told them, "No, I'm not letting Benjamin go down to Egypt! I've already lost Joseph, and now I've lost Simeon!" He was willing to let his son Simeon rot in jail rather than sending them all back with Benjamin and possibly losing him too. Finally, he conceded, realizing there really wasn't any option but to comply.

When the brothers returned to Egypt with Benjamin, they bowed down before him for a second and third time (Gen. 43:26, 28). Afterward, Joseph held a feast for them and released them. But before they left, he had one of his servants place a silver cup in Benjamin's sack. Then he accused his brothers of stealing it.

Let's pick up the story in Genesis 44:14–16. This is where Joseph's brothers bow down before him a fourth time:

> *"And Judah and his brethren came to Joseph's house; for he was yet there: and they fell before him on the ground. And Joseph said unto them, What deed is this that ye have done? wot ye not that such a man as I can certainly divine? And Judah said, What shall we say unto my lord? what shall we speak? or how shall we clear ourselves? God hath found out the iniquity of thy servants: behold, we are my lord's servants."*

Judah was basically confessing, "We deserve this. We are reaping what we've sown." He was coming to the end of himself, which is what had God ordained all along. Now, as a penalty for this "theft," Joseph demanded that

Benjamin be his slave—the one brother who could not be left behind!

Then Judah said,

"Now therefore when I come to thy servant my father, and the lad be not with us; seeing that his life is bound up in the lad's life; It shall come to pass, when he seeth that the lad is not with us, that he will die: and thy servants shall bring down the gray hairs of thy servant our father with sorrow to the grave. For thy servant became surety for the lad unto my father, saying, If I bring him not unto thee, then I shall bear the blame to my father for ever. Now therefore, I pray thee, let thy servant abide instead of the lad a bondman to my lord; and let the lad go up with his brethren. For how shall I go up to my father, and the lad be not with me? Lest peradventure I see the evil that shall come on my father."

Genesis 44:30–34

There are some really significant things right here. Judah was saying that if he went back without Benjamin, he was going to bring down his father's gray hairs to the grave, that it would kill him, and he would be responsible.

Now, remember that years earlier, when they sold Joseph into slavery, they didn't care how hurt their father would be. Jacob suffered every day for decades as these ungodly men watched. They cared more about themselves than about telling him the truth. Now Judah was offering to stay in place of Benjamin. He literally laid down his life for the sake of brother and his father. That's the greatest expression of love that there is (John 15:13). God had done a work in these men.

I believe this is what Joseph's dreams were all about. They weren't just about his brothers bowing down before him; they were more about them bowing the knee to God. Joseph was the catalyst God used to finally hold these men accountable and bring them to the end of themselves. This is what God wanted. This is repentance.

So, after Judah said he was willing to be a slave in Benjamin's place, the Bible says,

> *"Then Joseph could not refrain himself before all them that stood by him; and he cried, Cause every man to go out from me. And there stood no man with him, while Joseph made himself known unto his brethren. And he wept aloud: and the Egyptians and the house of Pharaoh*

heard. And Joseph said unto his brethren, I am Joseph; doth my father yet live? And his brethren could not answer him; for they were troubled at his presence."

Genesis 45:1–3

These men were shocked beyond belief that this man they had been dealing with was not only the second most powerful person in the world but also their brother whom they had sold into slavery! Now he had their lives in his hand. I guarantee you, fear and dread came upon them. What was going to be his response?

Joseph responds with compassion in Genesis 45 and again in Genesis 50:19–21, which says,

"And Joseph said unto them, Fear not: for am I in the place of God? But as for you, ye thought evil against me; but God meant it unto good, to bring to pass, as it is this day, to save much people alive. Now therefore fear ye not: I will nourish you, and your little ones. And he comforted them, and spake kindly unto them."

Joseph assured his brothers that he'd never held anything against them and would never take vengeance on them. So, again, Joseph did not have any animosity in his heart toward his brethren.

Psalm 105:17 says,

"[God] sent a man before them, even Joseph, who was sold for a servant."

Some people have taken these verses and said that all of the negative things that happened to Joseph were God's will. No! That's not what happened. God certainly used the hardship Joseph went through, but He was not the cause of it.

Lesson 23:
God can use the hardship you go through, but He is not the cause of it.

Romans 8:28 says,

"And we know that all things work together for good to them that love God, to them who are the called according to his purpose."

God can take everything and work it together for good.

Lesson 24:
God can take everything and work it together for good.

44

You could just as easily say that God used Joseph's circumstances to counter his brother's evil and save all of their lives.

Conclusion

If you are living in defeat and things aren't working, that's never God's plan for you. Up to this point, your life is basically the sum total of choices you have made. You're either reaping what you've sown or, instead of staying faithful and holding on to what has He told you, you've gotten into discouragement and have become bitter instead of better. Either way, God can turn things around! You can choose how you react to life's pressures or successes. If Joseph made it, then so can you. If you'll humble yourself, submit to God, and start seeing by faith the way Joseph did, you'll come out smelling like a rose.

1 Corinthians 10:13 says,

"There hath no temptation taken you but such as is common to man: but God is faithful, who will not suffer you to be tempted above that ye are able; but will with the temptation also make a way to escape, that ye may be able to bear it."

In other words, the same principles that applied to Joseph apply to you today. God has a purpose for your life. You may have already gotten a glimpse of that, and you're headed in that direction. However, you may be going through a period of time when nothing looks consistent with what God has put in your heart.

I encourage you to learn these lessons at Joseph's expense. You don't have to learn by hard knocks. Stay strong and encourage yourself in the Lord (1 Sam. 30:6). I pray that God will use Joseph's story to inspire you and help you see His plans and purposes for your life come to pass.

Lesson 25:
The same principles that applied to Joseph apply to you today.

Lesson 26:
Stay strong and encourage yourself in the Lord.

Receive Jesus as Your Savior

Choosing to receive Jesus Christ as your Lord and Savior is the most important decision you'll ever make!

God's Word promises, *"That if thou shalt confess with thy mouth the Lord Jesus, and shalt believe in thine heart that God hath raised him from the dead, thou shalt be saved. For with the heart man believeth unto righteousness; and with the mouth confession is made unto salvation"* (Rom. 10:9–10). *"For whosoever shall call upon the name of the Lord shall be saved"* (Rom. 10:13). By His grace, God has already done everything to provide salvation. Your part is simply to believe and receive.

Pray out loud: "Jesus, I confess that You are my Lord and Savior. I believe in my heart that God raised You from the dead. By faith in Your Word, I receive salvation now. Thank You for saving me."

The very moment you commit your life to Jesus Christ, the truth of His Word instantly comes to pass in your spirit. Now that you're born again, there's a brand-new you!

Please contact us and let us know that you've prayed to receive Jesus as your Savior. We'd like to send you some free materials to help you on your new journey. Call our Helpline: **719-635-1111** (available 24 hours a day, seven days a week) to speak to a staff member who is here to help you understand and grow in your new relationship with the Lord.

Welcome to your new life!

Receive the Holy Spirit

As His child, your loving heavenly Father wants to give you the supernatural power you need to live a new life. *"For every one that asketh receiveth; and he that seeketh findeth; and to him that knocketh it shall be opened…how much more shall your heavenly Father give the Holy Spirit to them that ask him?"* (Luke 11:10–13).

All you have to do is ask, believe, and receive!

Pray this: "Father, I recognize my need for Your power to live a new life. Please fill me with Your Holy Spirit. By faith, I receive it right now. Thank You for baptizing me. Holy Spirit, You are welcome in my life."

Congratulations! Now you're filled with God's supernatural power.

Some syllables from a language you don't recognize will rise up from your heart to your mouth (1 Cor. 14:14). As you speak them out loud by faith, you're releasing God's power from within and building yourself up in the spirit (1 Cor. 14:4). You can do this whenever and wherever you like.

It doesn't really matter whether you felt anything or not when you prayed to receive the Lord and His Spirit. If you believed in your heart that you received, then God's Word promises you did. *"Therefore I say unto you, What things soever ye desire, when ye pray, believe that ye receive them, and ye shall have them"* (Mark 11:24). God always honors His Word—believe it!

We would like to rejoice with you, pray with you, and answer any questions to help you understand more fully what has taken place in your life! Please contact us to let us know that you've prayed to be filled with the Holy Spirit and to receive some free materials we have for you. Call our Helpline: **719-635-1111** (available 24 hours a day, seven days a week).

Call for Prayer

If you need prayer for any reason, you can call our Helpline, 24 hours a day, seven days a week at **719-635-1111**. A trained prayer minister will answer your call and pray with you.

Every day, we receive testimonies of healings and other miracles from our Helpline, and we are ministering God's nearly-too-good-to-be-true message of the Gospel to more people than ever. So, I encourage you to call today!

About the Author

Andrew Wommack's life was forever changed the moment he encountered the supernatural love of God on March 23, 1968. As a renowned Bible teacher and author, Andrew has made it his mission to change the way the world sees God.

Andrew's vision is to go as far and deep with the Gospel as possible. His message goes far through the *Gospel Truth* television program, which is available to nearly half the world's population. The message goes deep through discipleship at Charis Bible College, headquartered in Woodland Park, Colorado. Founded in 1994, Charis has campuses across the United States and around the globe.

Andrew also has an extensive library of teaching materials in print, audio, and video. More than 200,000 hours of free teachings can be accessed at **awmi.net**.

Contact Information

Andrew Wommack Ministries, Inc.
PO Box 3333
Colorado Springs, CO 80934-3333
info@awmi.net
awmi.net

Helpline: 719-635-1111 (available 24/7)

Charis Bible College
info@charisbiblecollege.org
844-360-9577
CharisBibleCollege.org

For a complete list of our offices, visit
awmi.net/contact-us.

Connect with us on social media.

Lessons from
JOSEPH

To dive deeper into this topic, you may be interested in the following products:

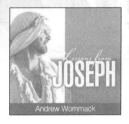

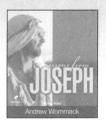

CD Series
Item Code:
1050-C 5-CD series
Suggested Donation $35

DVD Series
Item Code:
1050-D 5-DVD series
Suggested Donation $35

USB Audio/Video
Item Code:
1050-U
Suggested Donation $35

Order today at **awmi.net/store**
or call 719-635-1111.

Your peace doesn't have to ebb and flow with the tides of circumstance. Build your life on the solid foundation of the Word.

Visit our website for teachings, videos, testimonies, and other resources that will encourage you with truth for any situation and help you learn God's plan for relationships, finances, faith, and more.

"I was lost deep in the world. . . . I started seeking the truth, and through AWM's resources, I have been set free . . . including receiving miracles of finances when everything seemed impossible. I am at peace with myself. I thank AWM for sharing the truth, which has freed me to understand God."

— David M.

Be empowered to live the victorious life God intended for you! Visit **awmi.net** to access our library of free resources.

Teaching God's unconditional love and grace.

Andrew's LIVING COMMENTARY BIBLE SOFTWARE

Andrew Wommack's *Living Commentary* Bible study software is a user-friendly, downloadable program. It's like reading the Bible with Andrew at your side, sharing his revelation with you verse by verse.

Main features:

- Bible study software with a grace-and-faith perspective
- Over 26,000 notes by Andrew on verses from Genesis through Revelation
- *Matthew Henry's Concise Commentary*
- 11 Bible versions
- 2 concordances: *Englishman's Concordance* and *Strong's Concordance*
- 2 dictionaries: *Collaborative International Dictionary* and *Holman's Dictionary*
- Atlas with biblical maps
- Bible and *Living Commentary* statistics
- Quick navigation, including history of verses
- Robust search capabilities (for the Bible and Andrew's notes)
- "Living" (i.e., constantly updated and expanding)
- Ability to create personal notes

Whether you're new to studying the Bible or a seasoned Bible scholar, you'll gain a deeper revelation of the Word from a grace-and-faith perspective.

Purchase Andrew's *Living Commentary* today at **awmi.net/living**, and grow in the Word with Andrew.

Item code: 8350

ANDREW WOMMACK MINISTRIES

Don't miss
The Gospel Truth
with Andrew Wommack!

Discover God's unconditional love and grace and see God in a whole new way!

- ▶ Hear the Word of God taught with simplicity and clarity.

- ▶ Understand the true Gospel message and be set free from all kinds of bondages.

- ▶ Learn how to receive your breakthrough.

Go to **awmi.net/video** for local broadcast times or to watch online.

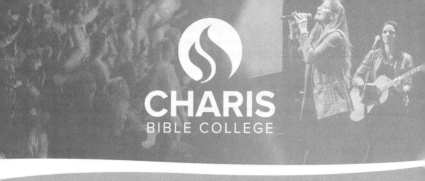

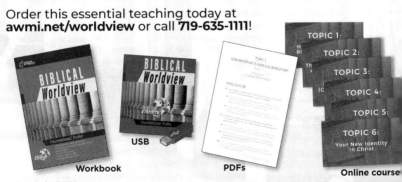